WILD FOX

PUBLISHING

Cover image: Sarah Morton – Sarah Morton Photography

Intext images: Sarah Morton – Sarah Morton Photography

First published 2023

Wild Fox Publishing, Scotland, United Kingdom

© 2023 selection and editorial matter, Sarah Morton.

ISBN: 9798373288590

Typeset by Wild Fox Publishing
www.wildfoxpublishing.co.uk

Whistle Stop Weekends: Isle of Skye

Pocket-sized travel guidebooks

Sarah Morton

Whistlestop Weekends Series

The Whistlestop Weekends series of travel guidebooks offer a pocket-sized selection of where to eat; drink; shop; walk; and, relax while in town. The travel guidebooks have been written from the perspective of being in a location for a weekend or a few days, and provide a selection of great options that have been tried and tested by the author(s) – all of whom have extensive, in-depth local knowledge of the area. The travel guidebooks are intended to offer genuine insight and suggestions for the places the author(s) love to go to, and would recommend to their friends and family, but come with the caveat that some self-directed research is also required ahead of travel. In addition to consulting this travel guidebook, you will likely find it useful to check, as examples, opening hours, some attractions may operation seasonal timetables, and travel to and from places, as this will vary based on how you plan to travel and when you plan to travel.

While the travel guidebooks are, by very nature, whistlestop guides, they are written by author(s) with a knowledge of the location so deep that they are able to write a travel guidebook from an insider perspective.

The Whistlestop Weekend travel guidebooks do not provide detail about how to travel to locations, other than a brief overview of some of the options for travel. We also don't make suggestions for where to stay while there. This information is much too fluid and changeable, and is also so individualised that it would be impossible to cover all options for all budgets, ensuring each to be as up to date as we can provide at the time of writing. We do however have a separate Whistlestop Road Trips series, and you may find there is a title in that series with information that is useful to you when you are planning your trip.

We hope you enjoy this innovative approach to travel writing and that our Whistlestop Weekend pocket-sized travel guidebooks help you to have the most wonderful time on your trip.

Making friends with the locals at Talisker Bay

About the Author

Sarah Morton is an intrepid explorer, she has loved travelling since a young child and has been fortunate to travel extensively for both work and pleasure. She has also lived in many cities and countries, and rather than scratch the surface she loves to immerse herself in the 'real' life of the places she visits. Sarah loves adventure, and spends a lot of her spare time walking, running, cycling, wild swimming, playing golf, and skiing. This allows her to experience more of the places she travels, going beyond the eating, drinking, and culture. Sarah is internationally published in books, journals, magazines, and online. Professionally, she is a design engineer and ethnographer, with specific interest in developing interventions for improving human health.

Table of Contents

Isle of Skye

Beinn na Caillich, Broadford

About the Isle of Skye

The Isle of Skye is perhaps one of the most frequently visited islands, both by tourists and Scottish locals. With the Skye Bridge linking the island to the mainland, it is one of the most accessible islands given it can now be accessed by road. It is still possible to access the island by boat, but travelling to the Isle of Skye by sea is now much less common. Accessibly aside, for that is not really why this wonderful location is so popular, it is down to the location itself. Located on the northwest coast of Scotland, the Isle of Skye is the largest of the Inner Hebridean islands. It is rugged, prehistoric in places, and beyond magical. It is quite impossible to put into words just how beautiful the Isle of Skye is, nor is it possible to fully document just how the island changes across the seasons, and even across the course of the day. There is the atmospheric, low-lying mist that blankets the island, then in a moment, it lifts to reveal imposing ridges and mountains; peninsula after peninsula of coastline; and quaint fishing towns. The sea too, surrounding the island, is equally majestic and unpredictable, from sparkling blue waters on the more sheltered eastern side of the island, to dark crashing waves on the more exposed western side of the island.

At just fifty miles long, and a relatively small drop in the ocean, the Isle of Skye may seem like the ideal Scottish island for a short break – and indeed it is, but it is worth taking a bit of time to soak up the island and enjoy the local culture, and perhaps go off the tourist trail and explore deeper into this richly historic island. The summer months can be frenetically busy with tourists and visitors. This is, of course, as with most of Scotland, the time of year when the weather can be most settled and therefore it is easier and more amenable to exploring the wonderful country that is Scotland. Large volumes of people on such a small island, can mean it becomes difficult to, for example, park your car at popular locations, or book a table at a restaurant for supper. With that in mind, you might wish to consider travelling to the Isle of Skye in the spring or autumn months. The weather at these times of the year can still be fine, sometimes even more so than during the main summer months. The Isle of Skye during winter is spectacular. Snow dusts the higher peaks and the passing weather can be breath-taking to watch from the comforts of an armchair carefully placed close enough to the log burner to keep you cosy, while peering out of a picture window, steaming cup of coffee or hot whisky in hand. An alternative to driving to the Isle of Skye, is to travel on foot or wheel, however, it is worth noting that public transport can be limited. By wheel / bike would be an ideal way to explore the Isle of Skye, but do check the ascent profile for any routes you plan to take while on the island – the Isle of Skye is not without its fair share of hills!

There are two main towns on the island – Broadford and Portree, and these are the most well serviced in terms of facilities, and have plenty of shops for essentials. There is more than enough to see and do in both or either or the towns for a weekend or short trip. However, it really is worth venturing deeper into the island – there are many famous place names with great attractions – Dunvegan, Staffin, Uig, Elgol, Kyleakin, to name just a handful.

The Isle of Skye is a place that is rich with culture and local traditions, and it is worth spending time getting to know more about the local crafts, the working landscapes, the architecture – both traditional and the more contemporary. The island also, as you would expect, has a rich and diverse history, and for those interested in such, the remains of the village of Boreraig is a site of historical importance since it reminds us of the Highland Clearances – which are a very poignant part of Scottish history. For those interested in Gaelic culture, the language is highly visible across the Isle of Skye, however, for some immersion, the Sabhal Mor Ostaig centre, which is the National Centre for Gaelic Language and Culture is the place to go – located in Sleat, on the southern end of the island, not too far from Armadale where the Mallaig ferry docks.

Know before you go

Weather and the seasons

Similar to most of Scotland, the weather on the Isle of Skye is as changeable in a day as it is across the four seasons. Because of its island location, it can be particularly susceptible to this. You could wake to a thick, low mist, only to have finished your morning coffee and be looking out to clear, blue skies with the type of sunshine that readily draws you outdoors. Unlike the cities, and less remote areas of Scotland, weather on the islands can be more extreme and this is true across the seasons. Often, a summer spent in rural Scotland draws visitors to become residents, only to find the winter to be long, harsh, and not quite what they were expecting. The key with the Isle of Skye, is to be prepared. This is not an island for your finest attire – unless you wish of course, or are visiting for a special occasion. Walking clothing and durable footwear are the preferred option, and to prepare yourself for the changeable weather it is good to have these options, particularly if you are planning to spend a good deal of time outdoors or taking part in outdoor pursuits in the local area. The important thing with travelling to the Isle of Skye is to not allow the weather to impact your plans. Watching the weather pass by can be such a spectacular experience, as can walking through wind and rain. On the greyer days, it can be a great idea to make your plans around the more popular, tourist spots – as they may not be quite so busy as they would be on a sunny day. Similarly, on a sunny day, it may be better to find a quiet beach or loch-side cove to enjoy a picnic. Or perhaps to enjoy some water sports or a wildlife watching boat tour. They key is to be adaptable.

Sunset, Broadford Bay

- **Summer** – the Isle of Skye in summer is just glorious, the days are long – expect to see daylight until close to midnight in June, and well into 21:00 and 22:00 in the earlier / later summer months. The Scottish love the longer days, and especially for those living in the north of the country the long summer evenings help to balance out the short dark days of the winter months. Generally, summers can be warm and mild with light rains, but there can also be cold, stormy days and nights. Scotland can be a very windy country, and even on the warmest day – the winds can be bitterly cold. Because the Isle of Skye is located on the northwest of the country, it can feel exposed to the weather systems, especially those coming straight off the sea, and on these days you may find the more sheltered eastern side of the island to be less affected. There are many parts of the island where it is very remote and there are limited options to duck in for cover if or when the heavens open – so it is a good idea to carry a waterproof coat with you. The Isle of Skye is surrounded by sea, of course, but also an archipelago full of other, smaller islands, and no matter where you are on this wonderful island, you will always be greeted by a spectacular view, and the light during the summer months, especially in the evenings, can make the surroundings literally dance.

In late summer, the hills are covered in blankets of glorious purple Heather — which is, without a doubt, one of the highlights of the summer months.

- **Autumn** — autumn in Scotland is spectacular and it is possible to see whole landscapes changing from lush green to golden hues of pinks, oranges, yellows, and browns. Because the days are starting to get shorter during the autumn months, the sunsets are beyond describable through the humble word. Less predictable can be the autumn weather, and while there are often many warm, balmy days in September and even until late October, if a cold winter is ahead, autumn can be grey and long. Because of the northernly location, autumn usually rolls in earlier on the Isle of Skye, and it can start feeling colder and more autumnal from late August sometimes. Wrap up warm though, and perhaps even use as an excuse to treat yourself to a beautiful locally knitted sweater, and enjoy crisp, autumn walks along the eastern shores and watch the sunset over the seas. Or for those hardier characters, stroll to the one of the beaches on the west of the island, and watch dark, stormy waves crashing onto black volcanic sand beaches.

- **Winter** – in winter the whole of the Highlands is cold, and the Isle of Skye, even though an island, is no different. Regardless of it being a mild winter or a hard one, the Isle of Skye is cold during the winter months. While one might assume, that a good down jacket, woolly hat, and thick pair of gloves will overcome, it is worth being aware of the challenges of moving around the Isle of Skye during winter. The roads can be icy, and sometimes coated with snow, which can make driving and travelling difficult. The mountainous areas, while spectacular, can also be dangerous places for those who do not have the correct equipment and experience. However, fully prepared, winter on the Isle of Skye is completely magical. Because of the height of the hills, there is almost always a dusting of snow, which is just so majestic and breath-taking. The light on the water is golden and inviting. It really is like being in a different world, and assuming you are fully prepared, it can be one of the most satisfying travel experiences you will ever have. During the winter months the days get shorter, so expect to see the sun setting from around 15:00, and always have a solid plan for returning to your base for your trip if you are venturing away from your accommodation. This is especially important if you are planning a walk perhaps to one of the local hills – ensure to have plans for returning before it gets too dark. Most locals will carry a torch with them in the event that it is needed to get home.

- **Spring** – spring on the Isle of Skye is, like most places with defined seasons, magical. After a long, hard, dark winter, there is nothing more relieving than seeing the days getting longer, the weather becoming finer (and sometimes warmer) and of course the vegetation blooming. During spring, temperatures can still struggle to get into double figures, and it is not uncommon to be in t-shirt and shorts one day, only to be digging out the winter fleeces and down jackets the next. During the spring months the Isle of Skye really comes alive – fishing boats start moving about again, farm animals begin to appear in the crofts and fields, locals too, who will have hunkered down for the winter, will be moving around again. You'll also see the local bird and wildlife bursting from every corner of the island – expect to see a wide range of sea birds, including rare birds and birds of prey, seals, sealions, otters (especially look out for them munching on a freshly caught crab!), deer, and many other, sometimes elusive, residents.

Otter eating a crab, Broadford Bay

Getting about while on the Isle of Skye

While Scotland in general is relatively well connected there is not a huge volume of buses and trains, especially out to the more rural locations, and most travel requires a bit of planning. Anywhere in the north of the country is best connected by road, and the most convenient way to travel is by car. For various reasons, this won't suit everyone – be it related to the environmental impact, or simply not having access to a car. Driving is on the left-hand side of the road, so do be conscious of the direction of the flow of traffic, particularly if you are unfamiliar with driving on this side of the road. If car is not an option, it is possible to travel by public transport, bike, wheel, foot – however, the Isle of Skye, which although accessible, is remote and there are very limited amenities en route. Do note that public transport can be limited, and self-directed researched is recommended if travelling by this option, as is careful planning of your schedule. However, it is worth noting that the train line which runs as far as Kyle of Lochalsh, on the mainland, travels through some of the most spectacular scenery in the world, and rail travel is a wonderful option for seeing parts of Scotland that even the roads do not reach. There is no train line on the Isle of Skye, so if travelling by rail, onward travel from Kyle of Lochalsh would need to be arranged.

Most access routes for walking, wheeling, etc., in Scotland are a mix of hard-paved tarmac and trail-type covering. It can be useful to do a bit of local research to ensure the covering of the route is suitable for your mobility needs. A lot of work has been taking place in and around the Isle of Skye to improve the active travel network, however, do bear in mind that it is an island location, and therefore facilities might not be the same as those which can be found in the larger cities. Examples of where access may be more challenging are paths to the beaches which may be along a farm track, and any of the hill walks including those which are on managed land, much of which can be narrow, steep and rocky underfoot. Also worth being aware that car parking facilitates can be limited, and again, work has been ongoing to improve facilitates at the more popular sites, however there are still some sites where there are just a few spaces to allow for car parking. While you may have driven some distance to get to your destination, it is important not to park anywhere that may obstruct access to, for example, a farm, field, business entrance, or of course, someone's home. Considerate parking is imperative — even if that means you must turn around and drive to a plan B location for your outing.

The Isle of Skye has three main ferry ports. The Glenelg to Skye ferry is located just south of the Skye Bridge. Take the turning at Sheil Bridge. The ferry runs every 20 minutes or so during the day between April and October. This is the last remaining manually turntable ferry in existence. So, it makes for a bit of a novelty to travel to the Isle of Skye in this way, and would provide quite an authentic experience as part of your trip. It is possible to travel by foot, wheel, or car. If you are travelling to/from Mallaig, which is a good option if you have been in the Fort William area or perhaps out on the Small Isles, you can cut out quite a significant portion of driving, and is no less of a spectacular journey. The ferry from Mallaig brings you into Armadale, which is in the south of the island. Sailings are year-round with the predominant ferry operator in Scotland, CalMac. The third ferry-based option takes you to/from the Western Isles, leaving from Uig in the north, again year-round with CalMac, there are two options to travel to on the Western Isles – Lochmaddy on North Uist, or Tarbert on Harris. Either of which would form a wonderful road trip. As with all ferry crossings, it is imperative to check sailing information before travelling. Weather can have a big impact on sailings in Scotland, and there are occasions when sailings are delayed or cancelled because of the weather. During the summer months when sailings are at their busiest there can be knock on effects caused by the weather and others waiting to travel.

Fishing at Broadford Bay

Local currency and language

The local currency on the Isle of Skye, as with the rest of the Scotland and the UK, is pounds sterling. There are many ATM cash points around the island, mostly in the towns where you can withdraw cash using an ATM compatible card. ATMs are normally located at a bank, at a Post Office, at fuel stations (garages) or mounted on a wall – known locally as a 'hole in the wall'. They are easy to recognise and are similar to use as those found across the world. To our knowledge, there are no bureau de change facilities on the Isle of Skye, however that is not to say the service is not available in, for example, a local hotel. It would be advisable to bring cash or a card with you that can be used while on the island and has sufficient funds for the duration of your trip. Ideally, the best approach would be to ensure you have all you need prior to leaving the city or at the very least prior to leaving Inverness or Fort William.

The local language is English, however variations of Scots may also be spoken by some locals in some areas. And in recent years there has been a Scotland-wide resurgence in Scots Gaelic. On the islands, Scots Gaelic is spoken more routinely than in the cities, it is now taught in many schools, and certainly, there is a good chance you will hear it spoken conversationally in say a café, or simply on the street. The more rural you go in the north of Scotland, the more likely it is you will become aware of Scots Gaelic being a key part of the local culture. You will notice that many road and street signs are printed in both English and Scots Gaelic, and this is something that is very prevalent on the Isle of Skye – many placenames have only a Scots Gaelic variation and there is a real drive to retain the Scots Gaelic language and culture. There are many places on the Isle of Skye where you can learn more about this if it is of interest to you, of particular recommendation is finding out more about the history of the Isle of Skye population, and how this has changed in recent years.

What to pack

Of course, what one packs for a trip anywhere is completely individualised and based on personal preference. As such, suggestions made here are simply to act as a guide for items that may be useful to bring with you on your trip to the Isle of Skye. As detailed earlier in this section, weather in Scotland and on the Isle of Skye can be hugely changeable and completely unpredictable. This variation can be from minute to minute or day to day. Layering is a popular option for being adaptable to the changing conditions and having easy access to those options that allow you to remain comfortable can make any trip to the Highlands more enjoyable. Scotland can also be a very windy location, and this is even throughout the year, so umbrellas are not often the most suitable item for getting cover from the rain, rather a good rain jacket / coat can be better at saving a windy and/or rainy day. For the most part, given the nature of most of the main attractions on the Isle of Skye, you will likely be out and about all day – so good comfortable footwear and clothing is an ideal option. Most locals are dressed for function and are adapted to the surroundings. The Isle of Skye is very much a place of work, as much as enjoyment, and you will notice that those who live on the island opt for a smart-casual look that is also functional. Most restaurants and bars have a similar dress-code, so unless you are attending a special event, the requirement to dress up in formal attire is not a requisite for most establishments – unless you want to, of course. Many establishments also have a walkers bar, which simply means you are welcome to come in even if you are head to toe in mud! Similarly, a lot of establishments are now dog friendly, meaning you can bring your dog(s) into the establishment with you – some will even offer water and treats for your furry companion.

Shops on the Isle of Skye are for the most part unique to the island and this is where you will find many special gifts and mementos of your trip – for both yourself and for others. You will find chemists, opticians, and grocery stores located in the main towns, but these are less well stocked than the equivalent in a larger town or city. They are also unlikely to open in the same way – so some might be closed on a specific day during the week, they may not open at weekends, they may not open later into the evening. So, if you forget an essential item, it could be that you find it is difficult to acquire what you need at short notice. Generally, if you are venturing deep into the Highlands, the Isle of Skye being a prime example, you will find that access to all sorts of amenities may be more limited. Stocking up on any supplies you need is best done while in Inverness, Fort William, or in one of the larger cities.

Friendly seal, seen from the Coral Beach

Where to Eat

While the Isle of Skye may be a remote, magical island lying off the northwest coast of the mainland of Scotland, it is definitely not remote in terms of eatery offerings. Quite often the perception is that there will be limited options for places to eat in island locations, the Isle of Skye is very much an island that blows that perception right out of the water. Surrounded by some of the cleanest, crystal-clear, and most abundant waters in the UK, if not the world, the freshest fish and seafood is on offer, as well as some of the most delicious land-based food from crops, to hand-reared farm produce, to some of Scotland's finest wild game. Again, the perception may be that all this amazing produce makes its way to the diners plate in the form of traditional Scottish fayre, and while this is certainly abundantly available on the island, you can also expect to enjoy some of the most innovative, contemporary and modern dishes. One consistent trend across the food establishments around the island is the intrinsic care that goes into cooking and plating food – quality and presentation are of upmost importance. While there is an unmistakable Scottish feel, there is also a very definite Isle of Skye identity that is present.

Where to Eat: At A Glance

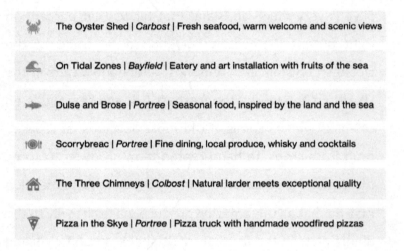

The Oyster Shed | *Carbost* | Fresh seafood, warm welcome and scenic views

On Tidal Zones | *Bayfield* | Eatery and art installation with fruits of the sea

Dulse and Brose | *Portree* | Seasonal food, inspired by the land and the sea

Scorrybreac | *Portree* | Fine dining, local produce, whisky and cocktails

The Three Chimneys | *Colbost* | Natural larder meets exceptional quality

Pizza in the Skye | *Portree* | Pizza truck with handmade woodfired pizzas

The Oyster Shed

Carbost, IV47 8SE

Located on the west of the island, The Oyster Shed is the perfect post-Talisker / post-Fairy Pools treat, and most especially if you are wanting to extend your day out by eating alfresco looking over the spectacular loch that is Loch Harport. In the case of The Oyster Shed, the word spectacular is not used lightly. This is perhaps one of the most scenic seafood sheds (sometimes called shacks in other parts of world) ever. It is not worth attempting to describe the view using the humble word – you will just have to go and see for yourself. Farmed in Loch Harport, the oysters available on the menu are quite literally fresh from the sea. You can also expect fresh lobster, mussels, scallops, crab, fishes such as mackerel, kipper, sea trout to name a few. And for those who aren't so keen on fish and seafood, there are other items on the menu including venison and chips. The Oyster Shed is open all year, and no bookings are required.

On Tidal Zones Oyster Table

Bayfield, IV51 9EW

Both eatery and art installation, the On Tidal Zones Oyster Table is quite a special concept. A collaboration between Atlas Arts, located on the island, and Cooking Sections, of Climavore, the table is located on the intertidal zones of the shores near the town of Portree. The underpinning ethos is one that considers the environmental impacts of intensive aquaculture. Each day the table is submerged under the ocean, gathering and collecting various species of oyster, mussels, and seaweeds. Then, at low tide, the table emerges and presents its collected fruits of the sea and provides an alternative take on alfresco dining. The sitting is different each day, since it is based on the tide times, and depending on when you visit, the table could be available to provide you with either your breakfast, lunch, or supper. Guided by Climavore, the meal is served as a performance and encourages consideration for taking care of the local waters, being aware of what we are eating, and the damage that may be caused by mass production of certain types of food. More widely, the Climavore project plays a key role in community development and the team have been working with local industry and children to develop opportunities within the local area. Given the nature of this concept, please check serving times in advance.

Dulse and Brose

Bosville Terrace, Portree, IV51 9DG

Located in the centre of the town of Portree, Dulse and Brose, encompasses, by name, true Scottish fayre. Dulse, otherwise known as seaweed, has been eaten by Celtic folk for centuries – from Celtic warriors going to battle, to the more recent diet of local crofters, dulse has been a staple. Brose is perhaps a more familiar taste – being more commonly known as oatmeal, or porridge. Again, eaten for centuries, by warriors and shepherds who spent long periods of time in the hills or walking along ancient drove roads to the south of Scotland and beyond.

Two typically Scottish ingredients, and an apt name for this wonderful, and truly Scottish eatery. Menus at the restaurant are developed seasonally and draw on locally sourced produce and ingredients. Think seafood platters, fresh from the local waters, wild boar sausages, hand-dived scallops, locally reared beef, and fresh salad from just a couple of miles away. Of course, there is an abundance drinks menu — including a dedicated whisky menu. Add to all that, a harbour-side setting and this is the ideal spot to enjoy a top-drawer meal, before an evening stroll to watch the sunset over the harbour. Perhaps you'll even enjoy a local whisky while doing so.

Scorrybreac Restaurant

Bosville Terrace, Portree, IV51 9DG

If fine dining with a view is your idea of heaven, Scorrybreac is the place for you. Again, located near the harbour in Portree, the tasting menu is divine. Starting with mouth-watering canapes, followed by a tasting size selection of fresh local produce — think, mackerel, chantarelles, Dunvegan roe deer, Douglas fir, finished up with a perfectly light and balanced desert and petit fours. The restaurant has recently been awarded a Michelin star, and it is so easy to see why – the food is the perfect blend of all that is modern Scottish cooking with French and Mediterranean undertones. There is a clear influence of the outdoors and the surrounding landscape, and the menu, so carefully considered, really does reflect this. Upstairs, there is a whisky and cocktail bar. The views across Portree harbour are spectacular, and there is nothing more wonderful that an evening spent here, cosily nestled into the sheepskin clad chairs and sipping a truly Hebridean drink.

The Three Chimneys

Colbost, Dunvegan, IV55 8ZT

If a restaurant is good enough to be recommended by the New York Times, then it's certainly good enough for us. The Three Chimneys is one such establishment. Located in the north-west corner of the island, this is the place to go for a real foodie treat or special occasion. Expect the menu to be abundant with local produce that reflects the dramatic and atmospheric landscape within which the restaurant is situated. Think natural larder meets the most exceptional quality — local oysters, Loch Dunvegan crab and langoustine, hand-dived Sconser scallops, Isle of Mull cheddar, and The Three Chimneys very own haggis fused with shallots, seaweed vinegar, roe parfait, Douglas fir, brown butter, tattie scones, or whipped potatoes. The mouth waters. The restaurant also runs a 'Kitchen Table' concept where diners can enjoy a communal dining experience for up to eight guests. Immersed within the busy kitchen, you can expect to experience the performance of the chefs and waiters at work. At the 'Kitchen Table' you will be offered a tasting menu which comprises dishes from land and sea — a concept which, in our opinion, completely sums up the Isle of Skye, for it is the ultimate location that encompasses all that is of the land and of the sea.

Pizza in the Skye

Portree, IV51 9EG

After a long, busy day of exploring the Isle of Skye and working up an appetite, there really is nothing more satisfying than ordering a freshly prepared, woodfired pizza. The Pizza in the Skye concept is very innovative and modern – text your order in, get a confirmation text with pick up time, and head to the pizza van to pick up your well-earned, and very tasty pizza(s). It's the perfect way to order food en route back to your accommodation after your day out. The selection of toppings is excellent – with some seasonal variations, and the quality is second to none, in fact – it's artisanal! At the time of writing, Pizza in the Skye indicated they were closed over the winter season – with opening again being from spring through to late autumn.

Where to Drink

The Isle of Skye, like many of the hamlets, villages, towns, cities, and islands of Scotland, have more places to meet for a drink than you can shake a stick at. Similar to many of the pubs and bars in Scotland, you can enjoy a drink or two, as well as some wonderful grub, if you so wish. With that in mind, many of the establishments suggested here also double as great places to eat. The suggestions in this section really only scratch the surface of meeting places on the island, and serve more as a starting point to some of the great places on the Isle of Skye. Each of the suggestions offered in this guidebook sit alongside equally wonderful establishments. So abundant are the offerings, that a guidebook dedicated just to 'where to drink' would be completely feasible! In essence, no matter where you chose to enjoy a drink during your trip to the Isle of Skye – you will not be disappointed. The culture across the island is warm and welcoming, and many of the pubs and bars have picture windows to allow you to enjoy the outdoors and watch the ever-changing weather and light from the comfort of a cosy, tweed-clad armchair, even more inviting during the winter months when the log fire is also roaring. In addition to the opportunity to sample a wide and wonderful selection of drinks, including local whisky and gins, you can expect to enjoy live music across the week, some of which will be of traditional origin – which is a real treat in itself. One thing to bear in mind is the proximity of some of the establishments, many will be within walking distance of your accommodation. However, some are located in remote areas and corners of the island. Public and private (i.e. taxi) transport may not be easily accessible, and that might be because of the time of year – if it is out of the normal tourist season perhaps, or if it as at the height of the tourist season, transport might be at capacity. This is an important point to consider if you are planning to visit one of the more remote establishments, or one that is distant from your accommodation. Drinking alcohol and driving in Scotland is not tolerated in the same way that it might be in other parts of the world, so, if applicable and you are the designated driver, please do check the Scottish rules and regulations in this context when planning your trip.

Where to Drink: At A Glance

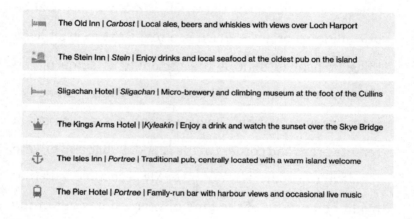

The Old Inn | *Carbost* | Local ales, beers and whiskies with views over Loch Harport

The Stein Inn | *Stein* | Enjoy drinks and local seafood at the oldest pub on the island

Sligachan Hotel | *Sligachan* | Micro-brewery and climbing museum at the foot of the Cullins

The Kings Arms Hotel | |*Kyleakin* | Enjoy a drink and watch the sunset over the Skye Bridge

The Isles Inn | *Portree* | Traditional pub, centrally located with a warm island welcome

The Pier Hotel | *Portree* | Family-run bar with harbour views and occasional live music

The Old Inn
Carbost, IV47 8SR

Located on the west side of the island, toward the famous Talisker area, The Old Inn is nestled on the shores of the sheltered, scenic, and atmospheric Loch Harport, in the small town of Carbost. Equally popular with locals as with those visiting the area, you can expect a true Highland welcome, so popular in fact, that you may need to book ahead if you are wanting to eat, as well as drink. A well-stocked bar offers local ales, beers, and whiskies. The traditional interior is just a wonderful spot to while away a rainy day in the summer, or a cold day during the winter months. On a fine day, at any time of the year, it is just delightful to sit outside, with a drink, enjoying the light and clouds dancing over the crystal-clear waters of the loch. Live music is also a key attraction at The Old Inn, with traditional Scottish through to modern rock music running throughout the year.

The Stein Inn

Macleods Terrace, Stein, IV55 8GA

Famed as the oldest pub on the island, The Stein Inn, with its wonderfully traditional interior, is tucked away in a pretty remote corner of the north-west side of the Isle of Skye. The crofting township of Stein sits on the shores of Loch Bay on the Waternish peninsula, with the Inn being perfectly located right at the waters edge. This is literally the ultimate spot to enjoy a drink while watching one of our spectacular west coast sunsets over the loch, and further north to the open waters of the Atlantic. A true 'on the edge' location. Sit on into the evening, and you might even experience the wonders of this dark sky location. The Inn itself is open late for drinks, and offers an abundant range of local and further afield options. Of course, the food is also great, and it would be criminal not to weave it into this section – expect to enjoy shellfish from the Loch opposite – think fresh langoustines, mussels, crab, and lobster. If seafood isn't your thing, also on offer is local wild venison and vegetarian options.

Sligachan Hotel
Sligachan, IV47 8SW

Located midway between the main towns of Broadford and Portree, the Sligachan Hotel is immediately beside one of the islands most photographed places – the Sligachan Bridge! If you are looking for a spot to take an iconic Isle of Skye photograph – this is the place for you. Surrounded by mountains, waterfalls, rivers, and quaint, traditional island buildings, bridges, and roads the Sligachan Hotel is an Isle of Skye institution. It's also in a great location since it sits at a junction of some of the main roads on the island, which makes it a very natural meeting point. More than a hotel, there is an on-site micro-brewery – the aptly named Cuillin Brewery, so if you are into the whole craft beer movement, you will likely enjoy sampling the home-brewed delights. For those with an interest in climbing, you might enjoy visiting the small climbing museum which houses artefacts dating back to the 1800s. Given the location, at the foot of the main climbing area of the Cuillin Mountains, this is the pub that draws in walkers, climbers, and mountaineers, and has done since it has opened. Which makes it a very special part of the Isle of Skye history and culture, and one that is highly recommended to experience during your trip – regardless of your own relationship with the mountains.

Who knows – you may even feel inspired to take up a new hobby after visiting!

Kings Arms Hotel

King Street, Kyleakin, IV41 8PH

Perfectly located just a few minutes from the Skye Bridge, the Kings Arms Hotel is a wonderful place to watch the sunset over the bridge! Which is literally nothing short of spectacular, in fact, it is surely up there with one of the best sunsets in the world! The Kings Arms Hotel is something that is a bit of a hidden gem, given it is located really at the main entrance / exit to the island, it can easily be overlooked in favour of whatever is happening further north on the island and indeed in the main towns of Broadford and Portree. The hotel itself is one of the oldest on the island, dating back to the 1600s, and as such, oozes traditional charm and atmosphere. Enjoy your drink with views over the water, on a warm evening or cosy up inside in the comforting confines of a comfortable, tweed-clad armchair beside a cracking, open log fire.

The Isles Inn

Somerled Square, Portree, IV51 9EH

The Isles Inn is a traditional Isle of Skye pub located in the centre of the town of Portree. A great central location – both for Portree and the island as a whole. Staff are dressed in the family tartan, and you can expect a warm island welcome. This cosy island pub is a favourite with locals, not just for the great service, but for the lovely atmosphere within which to enjoy a drink or two. Nestle yourself by the fireplace to warm up on one of the colder days. The Isles Inn is family and dog friendly.

Pier Hotel

Quay Street, Portree, IV51 9DE

Located right on the harbour overlooking Portree Bay, the views from the Pier Hotel are quite simply stunning. Whether shrouded in low mist or bathed in glorious

Scottish sunshine, it will be difficult to peel yourself away from the view out of the window. The Pier Hotel is a family-run establishment, and you can expect a true warm welcome the moment you walk through the door. The bar offers a range of drinks, including local beers and whiskies, and time your trip correctly, and you might also get to enjoy an evening of traditional live music.

Isle of Skye sunset

Where to Shop

Shopping is perhaps not on the top of the agenda when planning a trip to the Isle of Skye. However, the Isle of Skye is a wonderful mecca for locally crafted goods with literally something for everyone. Whether you are shopping for some authentic souvenirs and gifts to take back to those at home, or perhaps you are looking for some contemporary Isle of Skye arts and crafted goods there truly is an abundance of offerings. Within the main towns, there are many outlets, housed within quaint storefronts. Outside of the towns, there are standalone outlets, often selling handmade and handcrafted items from the very workshop or studio where they were made. The Isle of Skye offers endless possibilities to purchase items that are truly local and unique – many of which have been inspired by the land and sea surrounding the island. Allowing you to take home a piece of the Isle of Skye for yourself.

Where to Shop: At A Glance

Sandbank Studio | *Broadford* | Artist studio with mixed media landscape paintings

Skye Skins | *Waternish* | Family-owned sheepskin tannery with a contemporary edge

Skye Candle Co. | *Broadford* | Family-run candle workshop – natural and hand poured

Skye Weavers | *Glendale* | Wool and tweed produced using a bicycle powered loom

Skye Soap Co. | *Portree* | Family-run company producing natural beauty products

Hebridean Isles Trading Co. | *Edinbane* | Working croft producing wool and knitwear

Sandbank Studio

Old Pier Road, Broadford, IV49 9AE

Run by local artist Duncan Currie, Sandbank Studio is located in a small wooden building on the shores of Broadford Bay. Specialising in mixed media landscape paintings, Sandbank Studio is a little mecca of wonderful artworks that will allow you to bring a piece of the Isle of Skye home with you. Duncan is equally delightful, it is always wonderful to have the opportunity to speak with an artist at their studio, and Duncan has always been more than happy to talk through his work. At the Studio, you can purchase originals and prints, as well as some smaller items such as bags with prints on and notelet cards. Duncan is a keen recreational fisherman, and will certainly be a great point of knowledge if you would like to do some fishing during your trip to the Isle of Skye.

Skye Skyns

17 Lochbay, Waternish, IV55 8GD

Skye Skyns is an Isle of Skye business that has gone from strength to strength over the years, and has really evolved the art of sheepskin tannery into a true contemporary craft. In fact, it is the only sole remaining commercial woolskin tannery in Scotland. There is nothing more luxurious on a cold winters day than sinking into a good quality, ethically produced sheepskin. Farming is big business across Scotland, and is one of the main forms of income generation for many Scottish communities. It's a way of life, and by making use of all of the animal through the production of high quality, sustainable goods there is a part to play in caring for the local environment. Skye Skyns has a tannery that you can visit, as well as a showroom, shop in Portree, and with many of the items being used as part of the interior design features of holiday accommodation across the island, and indeed Scotland, you might even have the opportunity to try these wonderful sheepskins prior to purchasing for yourself. In addition to sheepskins and sheepskin home accessories, Skye Skyns also sell a wonderful range of woollen and tweed items, boots and slippers, and Skye seaglass jewellery.

Isle of Skye Candle Company

Old Post Office Yard, Broadford, IV49 9AB

The Isle of Skye Candle Company is a family-run workshop where the candles are blended and hand-poured in the town of Broadford. Each candle is carefully handcrafted from the finest natural and sustainable ingredients, all of which have a heavenly scent inspired by nature. The brand itself is built on an ethos of being considerate to the environment and being aware of the environmental impact that products can have on everything that surrounds us. So, by buying from the Isle of Skye Candle Company you can be sure you are also doing your bit for preserving our beautiful world, as well as enjoying a wonderful item made on the Isle of Skye. In terms of scents, you can expect a real local feel, think Bog Myrtle, Highland Gorse, Scots Pine, Heather, as well as the more exotic, such as, Rose, Sandalwood, Ginger, and Oriental Lily. If candles are not your thing, the Isle of Skye Candle Company also offer a range of beautiful skin care items and some little 'extras' including a small clothing line.

Skye Weavers

18 Fasach, Glendale, IV55 8WP

Located on the northwest of the island, on the Duirinish peninsula, Skye Weavers use a bicycle powered loom to weave their wonderful woollen creations, including blankets, throws, and scarves. They are also a tweed maker and sell lengths of this traditional Scottish fabric for making into various garments, homewares, and other items that can be made from tweed. It is possible to watch the weavers at work, which is just wonderful and a great way to experience this traditional craft and of course the making of such an iconic fabric. There is also an onsite shop, where you can purchase the full range of items manufactured by the Skye Weavers, and really does make a very unique gift to bring home with you. As we become more conscious of where our clothing and homewares come from, and how they are produced, Skye Weavers also offers the opportunity to purchase an item that is ethical, environmentally conscious, and sustainable – these are items that will last you for years to come, and perhaps you will even hand them down as heirlooms!

The Isle of Skye Soap Company

Somerled Square, Portree, IV51 9EH

Located in the main town of Portree, the Isle of Skye Soap Company is a perfect place to pick up some heavenly scented items to remind you of your trip to Skye if you are just on the island for a short trip and won't be able to, or don't have time to, venture deeper into the island and enjoy those outlets that are a bit more off the beaten track. In line with the ethos, you would expect of any beauty products produced on the island, the Isle of Skye Soap Company offers products that are handcrafted, using the purest essential and aromatherapy oils. Additionally, the oils used are plant-based – which is believed to be better for the skin. The family-run business opened in 2000 and has been a thriving cottage industry that reflects all that is the Isle of Skye, albeit in soap format! Visit the shop to stock up your bathroom shelves with soaps, melts, oils, candles, creams, lotions, and potions – all of which are inspired by the local environment of mountains, seas, lochs, rivers, and big skies.

Hebridean Isles Trading Company

Eilean Oir, 1 A Edinbane, IV51 9PR

Located on the north of the island, on the road to Dunvegan, the Hebridean Isles Trading Company, also going by the name of Island at the Edge, is a great place to add in to your visit to the north / north east of the Isle of Skye. This working croft (small Highland farm) offers an opportunity to learn about sheep and sheep rearing, shearing of the wool, right through to the spinning and crafting the spun wool into knitted items and garments. With, of course, the opportunity to purchase some of the wonderful handcrafted items for yourself, which includes tweeds made on the croft. In addition to being able to learn about the process, the Hebridean Isles Trading Company also offer teaching, to allow you to learn traditional knitting, crocheting, and land-based skills. It is an ideal place to visit if you are interested in crofting or smallholding, or of course, wool-based crafts.

Hebridean lamb

Where to Walk

The Isle of Skye is an iconic location for walking, with more options than you could ever cover in short trip – or perhaps even a lifetime. The options are endless actually, and there is everything from challenging and technical climbing and scrambling, to long-distance trails, to more mellow coastal paths. Many of the more technical routes do require at the very least some degree of mountain skill, and it is important to do your research if you are planning to include these in your travel itinerary. The Isle of Skye is one of the most beautiful places on earth, and there is much to explore on foot. In recent years, there has been work to improve the trail and path infrastructure, including strategies to accommodate those with accessibility needs. However, many of the walking routes on the Isle of Skye are on trails that can be narrow and steep in places, and with the increase in tourism in the past ten years or so, there is also much erosion of some paths, making them even more difficult for those with accessibility needs. As such, the routes described here are detailed with as much recent information as possible in terms of accessibility and what you can expect when you get there. But do bear in mind that there may be changes to access and/or changes to the terrain or paths since the time of writing, so please do conduct some self-directed research before heading out to ensure the route is right for you. If you are wheeling, be it wheelchair, bike, scooter, please also check the terrain suits your mode of transport. Any accessibility limitations are highlighted where possible and where known at the time of writing. The Isle of Skye is a rural island, and some routes may not be suitable for those with accessibly needs so the terrain and any special considerations are detailed as much as possible and based on most recent knowledge to allow for an informed decision to be made about the accessibly of each of the routes. Types of footwear and any additional equipment is down to individual responsibility and some awareness of needs and requirements would be beneficial for more remote and higher-level routes. The island itself offers wonderful walking – just to wander, or to experience those places you have seen in photos – there is so much land and sea to take in. The Isle of Skye has a very special energy, and taking time to soak that up is an essential on your trip. Simply being in the landscape and being part of the island, even just for a short while, is a great way of absorbing the energy of this wonderful and magical island.

Where to Walk: At A Glance

Fairy Pools | *Glenbrittle* | Crystal-clear mountain pools with the Black Cullins above

Old Man of Storr | *Trotternish* | Iconic rocky pillar rising out of prehistoric landscape

Coral Beach | *Claigan* | Secluded beach covered in tiny coloured coral, with great views

Talisker Bay | *Talisker* | Gray sandy beach with dark crashing waves and views to the isles

An Corran Beach | *Garrafad* | Dinosaur footprints, rugged and remote landscape and cliffs

Kilt Rock | *Staffin* | Towering basalt columns and haunting waterfall songs

The Fairy Pools

Glenbrittle, IV47 8TA

The Fairy Pools are perhaps one of the most visited and photographed locations on the Isle of Skye. In recent years they have become a very popular tourist location, and one that no good travel guidebook could omit! Located in the east of the island, with the imposing Black Cuillins in the backdrop, the Fairy Pools are the most crystal-clear blue mountain pools. If you're brave enough – you might even venture in for a cold water 'wild swim'. The walk itself is out and back from the carpark at Glumagan Na Sithichean, and the path is mountainous trail – bear in mind this is at the foot of one of the most challenging mountain ranges in Scotland. The terrain might not be suitable for all, and certainly care is required if there has been rain or wintery conditions. There are also some river crossings, which are great fun – but again can become challenging if there has been a lot of rainfall recently. There are a number of waterfalls to see along the river and deeper into the hills, if you don't want a very long walk, it is possible to walk to the first waterfall and return from there. Which is no less of an experience, given it is all truly magical. It is worth bearing in mind that as this is one of the most popular sights on the Isle of Skye it can become very busy during peak tourist season and therefore it can be difficult to get parked.

The Old Man of Storr

Trotternish, IV51 9HX

Another iconic landmark on the Isle of Skye, and indeed of Scotland, is the Old Man of Storr - a rocky pillar rising out of the imposing and rugged hillside. Located in the north end of the island on the Trotternish peninsula, the Old Man of Storr is a challenging, uphill walk that has become extremely popular in recent years. Assuming you get a good day, the views and being immersed in such mystical landscape make the effort worthwhile. Even in poor weather, it makes a wonderful experience – there is nothing more atmospherically Scottish than being in the hills with low cloud and mist swirling around you. The Old

Man of Storr is another very busy location during peak tourist season and although there is a good car park at the site, it can be difficult to get parked at busy times. The trail may not be accessible for all.

Coral Beach

Claigan, IV55 8WF

Located in the northeast of the Isle of Skye, just north of the village and castle of Dunvegan, the Coral Beach does exactly what it says on the tin! This secluded beach is covered in tiny pieces of pastel coloured coral. Coral being crushed skeletons of Red Coralline seaweed, also known as Maerl. Perhaps trickier to get to, given there is a substantial section of the drive along a single-track road, but the walk out to the beach is much more accessible than some of the other routes detailed in this book, albeit on wide farm track and with a need for off-road wheels, however, is relatively flat and easy going terrain. Although the Coral Beach is also a popular tourist spot, it is generally much less busy than some of the other areas, and even when busy, it is quite open and therefore possible to feel there is more space around you! The views across Loch Dunvegan, west toward the Western Isles, and immediately north to the small uninhabited island of Isay are just spectacular on a clear day. This is an ideal place to come and watch the sunset, and if you keep a close eye on the water, you may even spot some friendly, playful seals.

Walk to the Coral Beach

Talisker Bay

Talisker, IV47 8SF

Located right on the eastern edge of the Isle of Skye, describing Talisker Bay is perhaps quite difficult – it is so spectacular, magical, and at times hauntingly atmospheric it is difficult to find words that truly capture this wonderful place. Standing on the grey volcanic sandy beach looking out at the vastness of sea, with the Western Isles in the distance it is truly awakening to realising the next real expanse of land beyond the Inner and Outer Hebrides is America! The exposed situation of the Bay means the dark waves quite often roll high and crash over the shore – which provides a very different experience to that of the more sheltered western side of the island. The parking point for Talisker Bay is located at the small hamlet of Talisker, there is limited space for parking, so do take care not to block or obstruct any entry points that may cause issues for locals. From here, the path to the beach is well signed and along a relatively flat farm track, making it accessible for those wheeling assuming use of off-road wheels. It is possible to explore around the Bay, toward the sea stack, the waterfall, and the high cliffs rising out of the sea. The best time to visit is at low tide – to ensure you get to experience the wonderful sands here. Another great location to watch the sunset.

Looking out toward the Western Isles from Talisker Beach

An Corran Beach

Garrafad, IV51 9JT

Famed for its 'Jurassic dinosaur prints' An Corran Beach offers the opportunity to see some 170 million (approx.) year old footprints that are believed to have been left from when dinosaurs lived on the Isle of Skye! The prints are only possible to see at low tide, and they can be difficult to spot if they are covered in seaweed or other marine debris. However, even in the absence of spotting any, An Corran Beach is just a wonderful place to while away an afternoon. Further along the road is Garrafad, and from here is it possible to walk out along the jetty and look back at the towering hexagonal basalt cliffs above the foreshore. These are the same rock formations you can see at Kilt Rock, and they are really spectacular when viewed from the sea. There are a number of walks from this area, ranging in distance and challenge, with information boards in the local area to help you select which is best for you and the try of terrain that best suits you. The access road to Garrafad is very much a single-track road with passing places, and is not the most driveable of single-track roads, with caution required and consideration for other drivers. The location can become busy in high season, however when there are few others around there is a real 'edge of the world' feeling with a great sense of remoteness that is a great reminder of this wild island location. There is parking, but this can quickly fill up during the busier seasons.

Looking back toward the cliffs at Garrafad

Kilt Rock and Mealt Falls

Staffin, IV51 9JE

Named so because of the rock formations of a likeness to the famous item of Scottish dress – the kilt. The towering basalt columns of Kilt Rock rise right out of the crashing waves 90m below. Kilt Rock alone is a spectacle of nature in its own right, however, this is the Isle of Skye – which truly is nature on steroids, and as such, here, you also experience the truly spectacular Mealt Falls. Crashing over the cliffs of Kilt Rock, Mealt Falls literally sings a ghostly song, and even more so when the wind is billowing through the falling water. An iconic landmark with excellent views out across the sea. For those with a penchant for adventure, there are stories of the falls freezing during the very cold winters and being used for ice climbing adventures. This is a very short and accessible walk, which can be lengthened by crossing the road and following the single-track lane for a walk or wheel part of the way around Loch Mealt. This beautiful freshwater loch feeds Mealt Falls and is a wonderful secluded spot to escape the crowds and enjoy some bird and wildlife watching, or perhaps do some fishing. The access lane does serve a number of houses, so do please be mindful of that.

Cliffs north of Kilt Rock

Where to Relax

Many places in the Highlands of Scotland can often be more associated with action, adventure, being outdoors, local food, as examples, rather than as places to rest, relax, and recharge. And certainly, the Isle of Skye offers all those things and more. However, there are many places on and around the island offering a more relaxing experience, and indeed many are hidden gems, that are perhaps more likely to be a local secret than found in the pages of a travel guidebook. And of course, after all the walking, drinking, shopping, and eating that you'll have done on your trip to the Isle of Skye, surely a bit of downtime, a moment of calm, catching your breath, will be more than welcome.

Where to Relax: At A Glance

Isle of Raasay | *Kyle* | Remote, rugged landscape with an abundance of activities

South Skye Sea Kayak | *Kilmore* | explore and soak up island views from the coastline

Highland Ceilidh | *various locations* | traditional Highland live music and group dancing

Talisker Distillery | *Carbost* | Oldest whisky distillery on the island, with tour options

Museum of Island Life | *Kilmore* | Step back 100 years to experience traditional island life

Loch Brittle Sunset | *Glenbrittle* | See a 'West Coast Sunset' over Loch Brittle and the isles

Isle of Raasay

Kyle, IV40 8PA

Lying just off the east coast of the Isle of Skye, you'll likely have seen the Isle of Raasay from a distance. Indeed, if you are staying in or near Portree – you'll likely have been looking right at it! Small in size, at just 14miles long, and 3 miles wide, don't be deceived – the Isle of Raasay packs a magical Hebridean punch. Perhaps even more magical is the translation of the name – the Isle of the Roe Deer. Although easily accessible from the Isle of Skye via the daily ferry from Sconser, once ashore on the Isle of Raasay, you will be immersed in remote and rugged landscapes that feel like you have been transported to the set of an ancient, Highland land. There's much to enjoy while on the island, including castle ruins, old railway lines, and the Isle of Raasay Distillery – which is part of the Hebridean Whisky Trail. For those looking to relax in the outdoors, there is an abundance of hill, coast, woodland and muirland walks, and certainly opportunity to enjoy sightings of the local wildlife, including the Raasay vole, deer, white-tailed (sea) eagles, golden eagles, seals, porpoises, otters, dolphins, and if you're really lucky – you might even see some whales!

South Skye Sea Kayak

3 Kilmore, IV44 8RG

Seeing the Isle of Skye from the sea is truly magical, it is really special to travel by kayak, or other small hand-powered vessel, exploring and soaking up the views of the coastline. There is so much of the coastline to see from the water that just isn't visible in the same way as from the land, and it really gives a different, slow adventure-style, perspective to the island. South Skye Sea Kayak run a great operation out of Teangue, which is (you guessed it) located at the south end of the Isle of Skye, on the Sleat peninsula. An area that is perfect for kayaking, or other water sports, given just how unspoiled it is, but also for the outlook the location provides toward Mallaig, and the most wild and remote of places – Knoydart. South Syke Sea Kayak offer a range of packages and options for beginners up to experienced paddlers, including half day, full day, and multi-day / overnight experiences which can include camping on a secluded island. The paddle guides are very experienced and knowledgeable, and whether it is a hidden cave you are wanting to explore by boat, or a specific type of wildlife that you are hoping to get a photograph of, the team will do all they can to make it happen for you.

Highland Ceilidh

Various locations around the Isle of Skye

If you haven't been to a traditional Highland Ceilidh, there's a good chance you will at least have heard about Ceilidhs. And if you haven't, well, let this be your introduction. This fancy word literally just translates to a social gathering or party with live music and group dancing. Ceilidhs are held all over the Highlands and while they may feel like a locals only event – everyone is more than welcome! It's a great way to experience some true local culture in your downtime, and perhaps hear some wonderful trad music, of which there is an abundance of across the Isle of Skye. There are many Highland Ceilidh events running throughout the year, and they will be advertised locally, so rather than list them here – since live music events are a moveable feast, with dates that change and locations that change regularly, the best thing to do is make enquiries locally and look out for posters advertising events that fit with the dates that you are visiting the Isle of Skye.

Talisker Distillery and Visitor Centre

Carbost, IV47 8SR

The Talisker Distillery, based on the very scenic shores of Loch Harport, is the oldest working whisky distillery on the island. Offering a range of tour options, including a distillery tour, a 'Made by the Sea' tasting experience, and a 'Cask Draw and Tasting' experience. Whichever you chose, you will be immersed in the distilling and production of the wonderfully crafted single malt whiskies produced for almost 200 years at the Talisker Distillery. The folk at Talisker don't just offer whisky, you can also experience some carefully curated adventures. At the time of writing, an annual, running in December each year, 'Taliskser Whisky Atlantic Challenge' was an option – providing the opportunity to row thousands of meters across either the Atlantic Ocean or the Pacific Ocean. For those with an interest in protecting the sea, there is an initiative to support rewilding of our oceans through the Parley Foundation.

Museum of Island Life

Kilmore, Portree, IV51 9UE

Step back in time for a short while and immerse yourself in the Isle of Skye life of residents from 100 years ago. At the Museum of Island Life you can spend time inside a traditional thatched Isle of Skye cottage that crofters would have inhabited with their families and animals. These modest cottages provided shelter and heat from an open peat fire. There is also a weaver's cottage, where you can get a sense of how traditional fabrics, including tweeds, would have been produced. The Old Smithy cottage gives insight into the traditional craft of farriery and metal work. Given all crofters at the time would have owned at least one horse, the smithy would have been a true community hub, with much hustle and bustle. Finally, have a wander through the Ceilidh House – which acted very much as a gathering room for the whole community to while away dark evenings through their own entertainment, such as storytelling, music, and singing. The same sense of community remains today across the Isle of Skye, however the Museum of Island Life is a wonderful place to experience the Skye life of old and develop an understating of the roots of the communities of this wonderful island.

Loch Brittle Sunset

Glenbrittle, IV47 8TA

At the end of the Glenbrittle Road, where land meets sea, you will find one of the most spectacular beaches from which to watch the sunset over the sea. Loch Brittle is a wonderfully enclosed sea loch, with waters lapping onto sparkling grey volcanic sand, which is just the perfect location to spend a fine evening. From the bay, it is possible to walk up into the Cullins, and there is also a campsite and a youth hostel, which means you can relax for the evening should you wish to. The view toward the Isle of Canna is just spectacular, and venture on foot over the headland south of the beach for views of the Isles of Rum and Eigg looking east, and the small island of Soay, looking south.

Glenbrittle from the Cullins

Afterword

Thank you for purchasing a book from Wild Fox Publishing.

We hope you have enjoyed reading our Whistlestop pocket-sized travel guidebook about the Isle of Skye, and that it has helped you plan for your trip.

Please have a look at the other books in our series - we cover a range of travel and lifestyle itineraries, across a wide range of locations and topics.

If you are interested in publishing with us, we would love to hear from you - please get in touch through our website: www.wildfoxpublishing.co.uk.

Index

ferry 15, 27, 55: crossing 28; port 27; manually turnable 27
fish(es) 35, 37
fisherman, recreational 55
fishing 55, 74: towns 12
foreshore 71
Fort William 27, 30, 34
freezing, falls 73
fruits of the sea 38
fuel station 30

G
Gaelic, Scots 30, 31
game, wild 35
Garrafad 71
gathering room 81
gin(s) 45
Ginger 57
Glenbrittle Road 82
Glenelg 27
Glumagan Na Sithichean 65
goods: locally crafted 53; sustainable 56
grocery stores 33

H
haggis 42
hand-poured 56
handcrafted 53, 56, 59-60
handmade 53
harbour 40, 51: Portree 41

Loch Mealt 73
Lochmaddy 28
loom, bicycle powered 57

M

mackerel 37, 40
Made by the Sea tasting experience 80
Maerl 67
Mallaig 15, 27, 78
marine debris 71
Mealt Falls 73
metal work, traditional craft of 81
Michelin star 41
micro-brewery 49
mobility needs 26
mountain(s) 12, 21, 49, 60: pools 65; range 65
mountaineers 49
Museum of Island Life 81, 82
museum, climbing 49
music 81: live 45, 79; modern rock 47; traditional 47, 52, 79
mussels 37-38, 48
National Centre for Gaelic Language and Culture 15

N

natural larder 42
New York Times 41
North Uist 28

wildlife 23, 77-78: watching 74; boat tour 17
wood-fired pizza 43
wool 56-57: crafting 60; shearing of 60; spinning 60;
spun 60
workshop 53, 56

Y
youth hostel 82

Space for your own notes about your trip

Space for your own notes about your trip

***

Printed in Great Britain
by Amazon

23249785R00056